JJ

Hundredth Birthday

Side and Front Views

James Joyce by Brancusi, 1929.

James Joyce's

Hundredth Birthday

Side and Front Views

A Lecture
Delivered at the Library of Congress
on March 10, 1982

by Richard Ellmann

Library of Congress Washington 1982

Library of Congress Cataloging in Publication Data

Ellmann, Richard, 1918-
James Joyce's hundredth birthday, side and front views.

Supt. of Docs. no.: LC 1.2:J85
1. Joyce, James, 1882-1941—Addresses, essays, lectures. 2. Joyce, James, 1882-1942. Ulysses—Addresses, essays, lectures. 3. Novelists, Irish—20th century—Biography—Addresses, essays, lectures. I. Title.
PR6019.09Z53323 1982 823'.912 82-600271
ISBN 0-8444-0408-X

The Gertrude Clarke Whittall Poetry and Literature Fund

The Gertrude Clarke Whittall Poetry and Literature Fund was established in the Library of Congress in December 1950, through the generosity of Mrs. Gertrude Clarke Whittall, in order to create a center in this country for the development and encouragement of poetry, drama, and literature. Mrs. Whittall's earlier benefactions include the presentation to the Library of a number of important literary manuscripts, a gift of five magnificent Stradivari instruments, the endowment of an annual series of concerts of chamber music, and the formation of a collection of music manuscripts that has no parallel in the Western Hemisphere.

The Poetry and Literature Fund allows the Library to offer poetry readings, lectures, and dramatic performances. This lecture is published by the Library to reach a wider audience and as a contribution to literary history and criticism.

Introduction

Good evening, ladies and gentlemen. It's my pleasure to welcome you to tonight's program, a lecture in commemoration of the hundredth birthday of James Joyce.

As few people in this audience need to be reminded, we've had something of a James Joyce jag in Washington this year, especially in early February when the actual anniversary of Joyce's birthday occurred. I had initially invited Mr. Ellmann to be with us at that time and to deliver this lecture on Joyce's birthday. His own schedule made that impossible — hence the five week delay. As you know, through the timidity of publishers and other causes, there were many delays in Joyce's life, usually measured in years rather than weeks. So our delay is merely emblematic of Joyce's career. But there are some ways in which this has been a fortunate delay. There was a lot going on during that week in February, including readings by the incomparable Siobhan McKenna, who was here for several days. I might add that during one of those days, she did come to the Library of Congress and recorded, for our Archive of Poetry and Literature, her readings of selections and excerpts from James Joyce. If we had had to choose in early February between an Ellmann lecture and a McKenna reading, that would have been for Joyceans a "painful case." In one other respect the delay has been if not fortunate at least interesting. As you know we are in the midst of the so-called Jupiter Effect. This has filled some people with dread and apprehension about tidal waves and earthquakes and other disasters. As the master of mythic and symbolic meaning, Joyce would certainly have been intrigued and probably quite gratified that this particular occasion occurs when some people at least think the earth is likely to stop spinning. I would have treated this subject more lightly if we had not had a fire and power failure on Capitol Hill today which forced us to close down the Library's Madison Building for most of the day.

Whatever date, Richard Ellmann was the inevitable choice for such an occasion. Although he has written widely about literature, his special province has been the great Irish writers of the past hundred years. He has made significant contributions to the understanding of William Butler Yeats, and he is nearing completion of a major study of Oscar Wilde. But it is with James Joyce that his name is inextricably associated. He has written about Joyce's writing, he has edited Joyce's letters, and in 1959 he published his biography of Joyce, which will be reissued and enlarged this year in a special centennial edition. Many people regard that biography as the beau ideal of literary biography, combining as it does the oil and water of exacting, comprehensive scholarship and astute and penetrating criticism. It also shows that appreciation for the genius of one of the greatest and most influential writers of the twentieth century does not oblige the biographer to overlook the personal shortcomings of his subject or to adopt a tone of advocacy and rationalization instead of scholarship and criticism. Ellmann's *Joyce* is the kind of book that everyone in this room would like to be able to write if only we knew enough and felt enough and worked hard enough to bring it about.

Mr. Ellmann was educated primarily at Yale. He has taught at Yale, at Harvard, at the University of Chicago, and at Northwestern. Since 1970, he has been Goldsmiths' Professor of English Literature at New College at Oxford University. It's a very great pleasure to introduce to you tonight Richard Ellmann.

John C. Broderick
Assistant Librarian for Research Services
March 10, 1982

II

Hundredth Birthday

. . .

Side and Front Views

THE WRITER WE HONOR THIS YEAR, of whom I propose to offer some side and front views, thought about his centenary long before it occurred to his readers to do so. James Joyce scrawled in a notebook on Bloomsday, the day of *Ulysses*, in 1924, "Today 16 of June 20 years after. Will anybody remember this date." His Stephen Dedalus in *Ulysses* asks the same question as he jots down lines for a new poem, "Who ever anywhere will read these written words?" Stephen also recalls, with a twinge, how before leaving for Paris he gave instructions that in the event of his death his epiphanies should be deposited in all the major libraries of the world, *including Alexandria:* "Someone was to read them there after a few thousand years. . . ." The library at Alexandria having been burned centuries before, chances were slim that anyone would be reading his epiphanies there at any time. Still, if Joyce mocked such immortal longings, it was because he had immortal longings to mock. His brother Stanislaus, who drew a sharp line between fiction and fact, remembered that James had given him similar instructions for the disposal of his poems and epiphanies before leaving for Paris in 1902. No one will object to brave youths displaying youthful bravado. Flushed with talent or its semblance, they have all claimed with Shakespeare:

Not marble, nor the gilded monuments
Of princes, shall outlive this powerful rhyme.

Sometimes they've been right.

Joyce was convinced that a great future lay in store for him, and on the promise of it he allowed people to help him secure it. In 1904 he thought briefly that the moment had arrived; an Irish American millionaire named Kelly seemed about to lend him money to start up a weekly magazine which was to be called the *Goblin*. Joyce said to his friend Francis Sheehy Skeffington, who was to be the coeditor, "I think I am coming into my kingdom." Unfortunately, millionaire Kelly withdrew. Eight years later the same phrase occurs in a letter from Joyce to his wife: "I hope that the day may come when I shall be able to give you the fame of being beside me when I have entered into my Kingdom." That he was still borrowing "left right and centre" did not dishearten him. In 1907 his second child was born in a pauper ward, but in that atmosphere Joyce confided to his brother, "My mind is of a type superior to and more civilized than any I have met up to the present." An empty wallet did not impede his conviction of spiritual affluence. His confidence persisted as he grew older, and his putative kingdom continued to include the posterity for whom he thought his books would be required texts. When Max Eastman asked him why he was writing *Finnegans Wake* in the way he was, Joyce replied, with a brag intended to provoke a smile, "To keep the critics busy for three hundred years."

The first hundred of these three hundred years Joyce appears to have weathered quite well. His books are indeed studied all over the world and have their effect even on those who do not read them. Anthony Burgess says over and over that Joyce has had no influence whatever on English fiction; he then contradicts the statement with novel after novel. If nothing else, writers in England as elsewhere have to choose when they start a novel whether or not to be traditional, when in the pre-Joycian past they could be traditional without scruple. Joyce does not lack for admirers; he does not lack for detractors either. His detractors are repelled by the Joyce fans who obsessively follow Leopold Bloom's trail around Dublin, or climb the stairs of the martello tower at Sandycove, or drink at the much refurbished bar in Davy Byrne's. Still, such activities are not more pernicious, or cultic, than climbing Wordsworth's Helvellyn, or visiting Hawthorne's House of the Seven Gables in Salem or Proust's aunt's house in Illiers. If Joyce particularly inspires such pilgrimages, it is perhaps because we long to be on closer terms with this *scriptor absconditus,* this indrawn writer, in the hope of achieving an intimacy with him which he does not readily extend.

Another reason for seeing the places described in his books is that Joyce, although he transformed them into words, did not invent them. He said, "He is a very bold man who dares to alter in the presentment, still more to deform whatever he has seen and heard" (May 5, 1906). This was in connection with the book *Dubliners.* He was always trying to verify details in the city which lay almost a thousand miles from the table at which he was writing about it. How many feet down was the area in front of the house at 7 Eccles Street? What kind of trees were there on Leahy's terrace? Some of Joyce's flavor comes as a reward for this zeal. For example, in *A Portrait of the Artist as a Young Man,* Stephen Dedalus, after protesting to the rector that he has been unjustly pandied, leaves the rector's room and walks down the long corridor. At the end of it he bumps his elbow against the door. I am told that generations of Clongowes pupils have bumped their elbows against this same door. Joyce attended so carefully to such minute particulars that, he claimed, if Dublin were destroyed the city could be reconstructed from his books. Its immortality would be assured through his. Other novelists are, however, much more likely to present a city in reconstructable form. Joyce offers no architectural information, only places to bump elbows, or to lean them, to see out of the corner of an eye, to recognize by a familiar smell. The city rises in bits, not in masses. Anything else would be travelogue.

He was at once dependent upon the real and superior to it. His attitude may be elicited from a story he once told to his French academician friend Louis Gillet. It was about an old Blasket Islander who had lived on his island from birth and knew nothing about the mainland or its ways. But on one occasion he did venture over and in a bazaar found a small mirror, something he had never seen in his life. He bought it, fondled it, gazed at it, and as he rowed back to the Blaskets he took it out of his pocket, stared at it some more, and murmured, "Oh Papa! Papa!" He jealously guarded the precious object from his wife's eye, but she observed that he was hiding something and became suspicious. One hot day, when both were at work in the fields, he hung his jacket on a hedge. She saw her chance, rushed to it, and extracted from a pocket the object her husband had kept so secret. But when she looked at the mirror, she cried, "Ach, it's nothing but an old woman!" and angrily threw it down so that it broke against a stone. For Joyce the story had many implications, such as that man was filial and woman was vain. But the main one was that a mirror held up to nature will reflect the holder's consciousness as much as what is reflected. He could quote with approval Pater's remark, "Art is life seen through a temperament" (May 16, 1907).

When Joyce was young so many subjects pressed urgently upon him that he had only to choose among them. As he grew older he needed more hints. He sometimes thought he must alter his quiet life so as to secure them. Of course he could say defensively to Djuna Barnes, "[Johann Sebastian] Bach led a very uneventful life," but when he was with Ernest Hemingway he discussed the possibility of going to Africa. Mrs. Joyce encouraged him: "Jim can do with a spot of lion hunting," she said. "The thing we must face," said Joyce, whose sight was bad, "is that I couldn't see the lion." His wife was not to be silenced: "Hemingway'd describe him to you and afterwards you could go up to him and touch him and smell of him. That's all you'd need." But the material he needed lay closer to home. For the main theme of *Ulysses* and of his play *Exiles,* Joyce could rely on an incident which did not happen but which he briefly thought had happened. A onetime friend claimed in 1909 that Nora Barnacle, in the days when Joyce was courting her, had shared her favors with himself. But when Joyce was actually writing his novel and play five years later, he had trouble reactivating the jealousy he had once felt so intensely. His wife complained to their friend Frank Budgen, "Jim wants me to go with other men so that he will have something to write about." She seems to have failed him in this wifely duty. She did however oblige him to the extent of beginning a letter to him with the words, "Dear Cuckold," with the helpful aim of sharpening his pen for *Ulysses.*

Joyce for his part made comparable sacrifices for his art. In 1917 and 1918 he was beginning to write the Nausicaa episode of *Ulysses,* in which Bloom ogles a girl named Gerty MacDowell on the beach. Joyce seems to have felt that he must do something similar. He made overtures to two women, perhaps with his book ulteriorly in mind. The first occurred in Locarno, where he went for a time to enjoy a milder climate than Zurich's. I learned about it through a coincidence. James Atherton, the Joyce scholar, gave a lecture in Manchester, and a woman in the audience came up to him afterwards and said she had a friend in Germany who had known Joyce in Locarno in 1918. He sent me the address, and I eventually got into communication with the German friend, who

James Joyce, 1919. *Courtesy of Richard Ellmann.*

proved to be a woman doctor—one of the first women doctors in Germany—named Gertrud Kaempffer. In 1917 Dr. Kaempffer was staying above Locarno, in Orselina, recovering from tuberculosis after having nearly died of that disease. Joyce, afflicted with serious eye trouble, was living at the Pension Daheim. One evening Gertrud Kaempffer came down by funicular railway to visit some friends of hers in the same pension. They introduced her to Joyce, who because of his three published books and his obvious intellectual distinction had a certain local celebrity. He took an immediate interest in the young doctor, and after some talk offered to see her to the funicular. But her friends whispered to her that Mrs. Joyce would be jealous, so Dr. Kaempffer declined.

They happened to meet next day, however, in front of the spa hotel near the casino. After some conversation he walked part of the way home with her. When she offered her hand in parting, he held it in his hands for a moment, stroked it, and told her how fond he was of such delicate skin, of such fine, slender hands. (She considered her hands to be only thin and sickly.) Gerty MacDowell—the object of Bloom's prurient scrutiny—has a similar "waxen pallor" and, as we are told, "Her hands were of finely veined alabaster with tapering fingers and as white as lemon juice and queen of ointments could make them though it was not true that she used to wear kid gloves in bed or take a milk footbath either." Joyce lent Gertrud Kaempffer *A Portrait of the Artist as a Young Man.* She was interested and asked his help with certain words which she did not understand. Joyce probably assumed that as a doctor she had much knowledge of the world, but in fact during her medical course her fellow students and professors had cosseted her as one of the first women students, and at the end of it she fell ill; so she was inexperienced and rather startled by the sexual overtures which Joyce soon made. She was fascinated by his mind, he indifferent, as she felt, to hers. When she would not agree, he asked her to correspond with him, and to use for the purpose the poste restante in Zurich. (Bloom also uses the poste restante in his clandestine correspondence with Martha Clifford.) Dr. Kaempffer reluctantly said no; she was put off by the idea of exchanging letters in secret.

Still, he occupied her thoughts, and she opened with interest the two letters he sent to her. Molly Bloom recalls how Bloom "wrote me that letter with all those words in it," and in *A Portrait of the Artist* Joyce depicts Stephen Dedalus's act of writing obscene letters and leaving them about in the hope that some girl will find them. With Gertrud Kaempffer Joyce indulged a kindred proclivity. Like Stephen's their correspondence seemed to be outside space and time, though it was not. He said he loved her and made clear that his love was physical. He hoped she had the same feelings. He said he wished to be entirely straightforward and to leave to her the decision about intimacy. Then, perhaps to excite her as well as himself, he described in his fastidious handwriting his first sexual experience. It had occurred when he was fourteen. He was walking with the family nanny near some woods when she asked him to look the other way. He did so and heard the sound of liquid splashing on the ground. Joyce used the word "piss," with which the young doctor was unfamiliar. The sound aroused him. "I jiggled furiously," he wrote. She did not understand this phrase either, but on later inquiry was told by someone that it was a kind of Scottish dance. In *Finnegans Wake* the principal character, Earwicker, is accused of having performed the same act opposite two micturating girls: "Slander, let it lie its flattest, has never been able to convict our good and great and no ordinary . . . Earwicker, that homogenius man, as a pious author called him, of any graver impropriety than that . . . of having behaved with ongentilmensky immodus opposite a pair of dainty maid-servants in the swoolth of the rushy hollow whither . . . dame nature in all innocence and spontaneously and about the same hour of the eventide sent them both. . . . " Joyce evidently recognized a farcical shamefulness in his own behavior. He confided in one of his letters to Gertrud Kaempffer another frailty: he found it particularly provocative when lying with a woman, he said, to be afraid of being discovered.

Gertrud Kaempffer did not regard these sentiments as fetching, and perhaps they were written more to indulge his own fantasy than in the hope of sharing it with her. She tore up the letters, in case anyone should read them, and did not reply. They would not meet again until a year later when, on her way to visit friends in Zurich, she caught sight in a public place of an unhappy looking, emaciated man, and moved closer to see if it could be Joyce. He suddenly turned around, recognized her and greeted her warmly, and invited her to a café. She could not go, having an appointment. Might she not come to the hotel later for a drink? Foreseeing embarrassment, she refused again. Joyce looked pained, shook hands, and said goodbye. All that survived of this abortive idyll was a recollection of having been aroused by a woman named Gertrud. At least he could draw one thing from it—the name of the young woman over whom Bloom excites himself in the Nausicaa episode—Gerty. As he had said in *Giacomo Joyce,* "Write it, damn you, write it! What else are you good for?"

He needed more hints for the episode than the aloof Dr. Kaempffer provided, and the second of his forays occurred some months after the first, this time in Zurich. We have known something of this affair ever since Prof. Heinrich Straumann of the University of Zurich obtained, just after the Second World War, the love letters Joyce wrote during it. More recently some details have come to light that make the context clearer. One day in 1918 Joyce looked out of a window in his flat and happened to see, in a flat in the next building, a young woman pulling a toilet chain. It was a scene that as we have observed had distinct erotic implications for him. He contrived to speak to this second young woman, whose name was Marthe Fleischmann, on the street. She had a limp, and he would give the same limp to Gerty MacDowell in the Nausicaa episode. He stared at her with amazement as if they had met before and was later to tell her that she looked exactly like a young woman he had seen many years before on the Dublin strand. Marthe Fleischmann seems to have coyly declined this gambit.

How far his feelings derived from the needs of his novel, and how far the novel from his amorous needs, were questions he did not have to answer. As he had written his brother thirteen years before, "there cannot be any substitute for the individual passion as the motive power of everything — art and philosophy included." (February 7, 1905) Joyce kept watching for Marthe Fleischmann and she, far from ignoring his attentions, closed the shutters of her windows. He wrote her an ardent letter in French, in a disguised handwriting, marked especially by his use of Greek *e*'s. He would have Mrs. Yelverton Barry in *Ulysses* complain that Bloom wrote to her "an anonymous letter in prentice backhand full of indecent proposals," and would have Bloom use Greek *e*'s in corresponding with another Martha. Joyce begged Marthe to tell him her name. She will not mind if he suggests she is Jewish, for after all Jesus lay in the womb of a Jewish mother. As for himself, he is a writer and at a pivotal moment in his life. His age is the same as Dante's when he began the *Divine Comedy* and as Shakespeare's when he fell in love with the Dark Lady of the *Sonnets* (a date we don't know). He is supremely unhappy; he must see her.

Marthe yielded to these importunities and agreed to meet him—whether she was Jewish or not. Joyce did not spend much time on religion; rather he turned the conversation to the congenial subject of women's drawers, always a titillating topic for him, and one which figures prominently in the Nausicaa episode. It was not easy for Marthe to meet him because, as she archly confided, she had a "guardian" named Rudolf Hiltpold. Hiltpold was really her lover, the man who paid her rent. He was vigilant, and she had to be circumspect. Joyce inscribed a copy of *Chamber Music* to her and left it in her letterbox. It was an appropriate gift for Martha, especially since he has Bloom in *Ulysses* reflect jokingly about the relation of chamber music to chamber pots. Evidently Marthe was impressed. Gerty MacDowell in "Nausicaa" would also be interested in poetry, though of an even more hopeless kind. Joyce now prepared a curious ceremony. On February 2, 1918, his thirty-sixth birthday, he arranged for her to have tea at the studio of his friend Frank Budgen. A note he sent to her that morning is headed "Marias Lichtmesse" or Candlemas, which also takes place on February 2, the feast commemorating the Purification of the Virgin Mary. He evidently wished to infuse a touch of mariolatry in his sexual approach, and in *Ulysses* he parallels Bloom's secular adoration of Gerty MacDowell with a men's retreat at a church dedicated to the Virgin. For the occasion Joyce borrowed a handsome Jewish silver candlestick such as is lighted during the festival of Chanukah and brought it to Frank Budgen's studio. He explained that Marthe would be arriving a little later.

Budgen had scruples about assisting his friend in this infidelity and said so. Joyce replied severely, "If I permitted myself any restraint in this matter it would be spiritual death to me." Rather than feel guilty of spiritual murder, Budgen gave in. There were further preparations. Budgen's paintings would do well enough as décor, except that there were no nudes among them. The painter had therefore to whip up a charcoal drawing of a voluptuous nude on the spot. Joyce said that in spite of his unwillingness to use given names, on this one occasion he and Budgen must call each

Arme liebe Marthe

Was haben Sie gehabt? ich Sie gesehen habe
Ich bin noch unsicher aber glaube dass ich wusste nicht wer
heute abend. Ihnen zu schreiben weil ich Briefe in die
Ich hatte Angst und dachte dass meine
bei Ihnen war kommen könnten.
Hände von fremde Leute
Jeden Abend habe ich geschaut. weil ich dachte
Ich habe mir sogar Vorwürfe gemacht in Folge einer
Dass vielleicht Ihre Krankheit letzten Abend war.
Erkältung auf [illegible] ich wollte Ihnen Vorgestern schreiben!
Dann dachte ich, ich einer Freundin schreiben!
und mit der Name einer l'allemand ne me va pas
continue en français parceque moi, j'ai
Si vous avez beaucoup souffert en ces jours,
souffert aussi l'unique rayon de lumière qui
Il me semblait que aux pères l'obscurité
dans ces dernières années
de ma vie était éteinte.
j'étais même imbécile! j'ouvrais le journal et
Chaque matin j'ouvrais, votre nom parmi les
j'avais peur de lire toujours avec
annonces des morts! je l'ouvrais lentement.
angoisse, très, très, elle qui m'a regardé
je pensais elle s'en ira — avec tendresse.
avec pitié — peut-être beaucoup. jusqu'au seuil de la
La maladie change quelquefois autrement.
Elle nous conduit les choses
mort: et nous voyons la mort — moi, si!
Vous n'avez pas peur de votre sentiment
Vous avez pensé, peut-être que vous avez
pour moi était une folie; l'au delà!
entrevu les ombres de ombres [illegible]!
les bien! Ce sont des ombres des fleurs mais j'ai
Je voudrais vous envoyer
peur. Peut-être ce n'était pas vous
J'attendrai encore.

que j'ai vue?
J'ai vu mon livre de poésies dans votre main.
Est-ce que vous avez compris?
J'ai senti quelque chose pendant votre maladie — quelque chose
de très amer qui a blessé beaucoup mes amis
Oui, j'ai souffert aussi. Avant de vous envoyer cette lettre
je désire savoir si elle tombera dans les mains d'une autre personne???
il pleut
Je vais jeter cette lettre à la boîte.
Je ne peux plus attendre!

J.

Letter from James Joyce to Marthe Fleischmann, late January 1929.
Courtesy of Richard Ellmann.

other not Joyce and Budgen, but Jim and Frank, and use the intimate form *du,* because he had spoken so often of Budgen to Marthe that she would find strange any more formal style of address.

Marthe arrived for Candlemas and Chanukah. When candles are lighted on Candlemas the priest speaks of them as symbolizing the light which shall enlighten the Gentiles and also the glory of the people of Israel. This text seemed to give warrant to Joyce's syncretism. He lit the Jewish candlestick ostensibly so she could see the paintings better, actually to lend a Judaeo-Christian glimmer to the erotic rendezvous. He toured the paintings with her, and as Budgen recalled, won a reproachful smirk from Marthe when he called to her attention the fat nude. Eventually Joyce took her home. He met Budgen later that evening and confided, "I have explored the coldest and hottest parts of a woman's body." Gerty MacDowell reproaches Bloom, "you saw all the secrets of my bottom drawer." Such scientific lechery would be mocked in the Circe episode of *Ulysses.* Presumably it remained exploratory, or so Budgen, knowing his friend's latent inhibitions, surmised. As for Marthe, she always referred to her acquaintance with Joyce as "eine Platonische Liebe." A day or two later Joyce was asked by another friend why he had borrowed the candlestick, and he replied, "For a black mass." Bloom, ruminating about Gerty, and at the same time remembering the words "Next year in Jerusalem" from still another Jewish festival, that of Passover, conflates the two in the Nausicaa episode by thinking how she "showed me her next year in drawers."

Further meetings with Marthe Fleischmann now became out of the question. The redoubtable "guardian" Rudolf Hiltpold got wind of the matter and wrote a threatening letter to Joyce. Joyce went at once to see him, assured him that nothing had happened, and gave him all Marthe's letters. Hiltpold was mollified. Still, Marthe's haughty, naughty beguilements helped Joyce to compose the Nausicaa episode, a point he confirmed by sending her a postcard with greetings to Nausicaa from Odysseus. Her limp, her coyness, her prattling about Platonic love, her responsiveness to his interest in drawers all went to furnish out Gerty MacDowell, whose first name and pallid hands had come to him from his earlier attraction to Gertrud Kaempffer. The assignation on the Virgin Mary's Candlemas, with Chanukah and Passover trimmings, would have its uses. His would-be infidelities had served his book, if not his peculiar life.

These two incidents give a sense of Joyce's seeking cues for *Ulysses* and, no doubt, for himself, by listening to songs of the Sirens. Still, closeness to life was not enough. I want now, a little more reverently, to inquire what manner of writer he thought he was. Granted that he believed himself from earliest youth to be an artist, it was as an Irish artist that he wished to become known. To that extent he was and always would be a part of the national literary revival. Although he spoke of *Finnegans Wake* as a universal history, the universe is given a distinct Irish coloration, and in a way the whole book is an arabesque on the Irish ballad of that title. Similarly his first work, now lost, written when he was nine, was on the most Irish of subjects — the death of Charles Stuart Parnell. In his youth perhaps his most passionate literary enthusiasm was for James Clarence Mangan, whom he complimented as "The national poet of Ireland" and as one who (he said) "had the whole past of the country at the back of his head," an ideal he marked out for himself as well. "An Irish safety pin is more important to me than an English epic," he remarked. Yet it was not Ireland as it had been that attracted him, but Ireland as it might be. Joyce was affected by the talk of renaissance that was in the air, and in the earliest as well as the final version of *A Portrait of the Artist,* that is, from 1904 to 1914, he ended by summoning in his imagination a new Irish nation.

The Irishness of his books was a distinguishing mark. *Dubliners,* he told his brother, was "a moral history of the life I knew" (May 5, 1907), and to his publisher Grant Richards he wrote, "My intention was to write a chapter of the moral history of my country." Joyce is often considered amoral; he regarded himself as a moralist. Stephen Dedalus concludes *A Portrait* with the words, "I go forth to encounter for the millionth time the reality of experience and to forge in the smithy of my soul the uncreated conscience of my race." Irony-hunters, who abound in Joyce studies, have been reluctant to take this expressed ambition of Stephen seriously. Joyce did so, however; in an earnest letter to his wife in 1912 he said, "I am one of the writers of this generation who are perhaps creating at last a conscience in the soul of this wretched race." His books move obliquely, even urbanely, toward this goal. In nine articles he wrote for a Triestine newspaper he presented his country's plight in more downright fashion. He offered these in 1914 to a publisher in Rome. They were not accepted: a pity, since they would have confirmed Joyce's "political awareness," a quality he valued in Turgenev. If he was not a nationalist of anyone else's school he was his own nationalist. His brother records a conversation they had in April 1907; Stanislaus argued against a free Ireland on the grounds that freedom would make it intolerable. "What the devil are your politics?" asked James. "Do you not think Ireland has a right to govern itself and is capable of doing so?" As an Irish writer, Joyce in 1912 went to the head of Sinn Féin, Arthur Griffith, to secure his help in having *Dubliners* issued by an Irish firm. Griffith, later to be Ireland's first president, was powerless to help but received him with respect.

As Irish artist, Joyce could be contemptuous toward his literary compatriots, whom he derided as serving lesser gods than his own. He was nevertheless modest before his own art. He had many of the self-doubts that are often attributed only to lesser writers. Though his first book was verse, he did not pride himself greatly on it and even denied to Padraic Colum in 1909 that he was a poet. Of course he did not like it when others agreed with his estimate; Ezra Pound was one of those who deeply offended him in the late 1920s by urging him to file his new poems in the family Bible. Joyce published them anyway but hedged his claim for them by giving them the title of *Pomes Penyeach.* He considered lyricism to be a vital part of his revelation of himself in his art, yet he played down his lyrics like a man unwilling to risk all on that throw. He was sufficiently affected by the criticism of early parts of *Finnegans Wake* to consider turning the book over to James Stephens for completion. As to *Ulysses,* he said of it to Samuel Beckett, "I may have oversystematized *Ulysses,*" though in fact Joyce had a Dantean skill in making what was systematic appear entirely improvisatory.

While he was writing his first book, Joyce owned up to uncertainties about the works with which he hoped to make his name. Of *Dubliners* he said to his brother, "The stories seem to be indisputably well done, but, after all, perhaps many people could do them as well." His autobiographical novel awakened even more misgivings. He had composed about twenty chapters of it under the title *Stephen Hero* when he abruptly announced to Stanislaus that he was changing the book's scope and redoing the early parts because they were not well written. When he had revised them, he was still dissatisfied. He decided to change it completely; instead of having sixty-three chapters, as once planned, it would have only five. He would omit all its first part, in which he dealt with Stephen before he started his schooling. Instead he would begin at school. The name of his hero, Dedalus, would be changed to Daly. Stanislaus roundly objected to all these changes. "Tell me," said his brother, "is the novel to be your puke or mine?" An even less savory metaphor of the literary art comes in *Finnegans Wake* when Shem is accused, this time by his brothers, of forming an encaustive ink out of his own urine and excrement, and writing on the only foolscap available, his own body.

The decision to make the book into five chapters was to stand. Otherwise, the new version pleased him little better. On December 15, 1907, he complained to Stanislaus, "The book begins at a railway station like most college stories; there are three companions in it, and a sister who dies by way of pathos. It is the old bag of tricks and a good critic would probably show that I am still struggling even in my stories with the stock figures discarded in Europe half a century ago." Stanislaus labored to reassure him. After all, there were not three companions, he said, but five. Sister Isabel died in the book because their brother Georgie had died in actual fact. Joyce conceded, "I didn't consciously use stock figures, but I fear that my mind, when I begin to write, runs in the groove of what I have read." This statement, recorded by Stanislaus, is the best hint we have that Joyce was determined to ungroove himself, to stand literature on its head. He did just that, and evidently he intended it from the start.

These remarks intimate what revisions he now made in *A Portrait of the Artist as a Young Man.* He eliminated sister Isabel from the book. No pathos, then. The opening scene at the railway station, evidently one in which Stephen arrives at Clongowes Wood College, is also left out. Joyce did not expunge Stephen's preschool days entirely, but he condensed them into three or four pages. The picture of infant consciousness, with shapes and touches and smells all distinct if not yet understood, and with words beginning to reverberate, was so astonishing as to provide

William Faulkner with the technique for the equally admirable portrait of an idiot's mind in *The Sound and the Fury.* After this overture we might expect Joyce to take up the narrative in a sequential way, but there are telltale marks that he is not doing so. We gradually realize that Stephen has a fever, and that what we have been reading is not a history but a deliberate hodgepodge of memories of his earlier school days and holidays at home, rendered with the discontinuity and intensity appropriate to fever. Not until two-thirds of the way through the first chapter does Joyce change the tense, and when he does so he is signalizing not only Stephen's recovery from fever, but Stephen's apprehension of his own distinctness as a recording consciousness. In *Ulysses* Joyce employs a somewhat comparable method by having Stephen recall the last two years of his life in a kind of fit, not of fever this time but of remorse.

Recent researches at Clongowes by Bruce Bradley have disclosed something more about Joyce's method in this first chapter of *A Portrait.* Although his own life provided him with much material, he ruthlessly departed from it where he needed. The first chapter culminates when Stephen, unjustly pandied by Father Dolan, protests to the rector. We know from Joyce's autobiographical recollections to Herbert Gorman that this incident was based upon fact. What we have not known until now is that this was by no means the only punishment Joyce received at Clongowes. The Punishment Book from that time is incomplete, but its surviving pages disclose no less than three other transgressions by Joyce in February and March 1889, at which time he was still only seven years old. He was given two pandies in February for not bringing a book to class, six in March for muddy boots, and four the same month for "vulgar language," an offense he would repeat with growing frequency for the rest of his life. Since these three punishments were presumably meted out with just cause, Joyce ignored them and dealt only with the great injustice inflicted by Father Dolan. So Stephen became a victim, and a heroic one whose protest against unjust pandying at a Jesuit school could be a prelude to his larger protests in youth against church and state.

During the year 1907 Joyce hesitated about keeping the name of Dedalus for his hero. If he had changed him to Daly, he could write the book on the same realistic level as his epiphanies and stories of Dublin life. Call him Dedalus, and he would have to justify the oddity of this name for an Irishman; he would be able to do so only by connecting the contemporary character with the mythical artificer of wings and labyrinth. Some years later Joyce would speak of his art as "extravagant excursions into forbidden territory," and in choosing Dedalus over Daly he made such an excursion. The result was that in the last two chapters, instead of describing only Stephen's movement outward from Ireland, Joyce represents also another movement, downward into myth. On a superficial level Stephen is dissociating himself; on a basic level he is achieving an association with Greek Daedalus, he is becoming himself a creature of myth. This decision led Joyce on to *Ulysses.* When asked why he had used the Odyssey so prominently in that book, Joyce replied, "It is my system of working." The method was established in 1907, when he threw Stephen Daly out and invited Stephen Dedalus in.

After he completed *A Portrait of the Artist as a Young Man,* Joyce had pretty well exhausted the possibilities of the artist-hero. For his next book he needed a new impulse. He was beginning to find it long before he used it, in 1907 also. In that year his remarks to his brother indicate that he was situating himself in relation to Ibsen, a figure he had idolized in his youth. "Auld Aibsen always wrote like a gentleman," he said, and added that he would himself not write so. On May 16, 1907, he commented, "Life is not so simple as Ibsen represents it. Mrs. Alving, for instance, is Motherhood and so on.... It's all very fine and large, of course. If it had been written at the time of Moses, we'd now think it wonderful. But it has no importance at this age of the world. It is a remnant of heroics, too." Joyce was very much opposed to heroics. "For me," he went on, "youth and motherhood are these two beside us." He pointed to a drunken boy of about twenty, a laborer, who had brought his mother into the trattoria where Joyce and Stanislaus were talking, while the mother was leading him home. He was hardly able to speak but was expressing his contempt for someone as well as he could. "I would like to put on paper the thousand complexities in his mind...." Joyce was obviously imagining the dense consciousness that he would give to his characters in *Ulysses.* He went on, "Absolute realism is impossible, of course. That we all know. . . .But it's quite enough that Ibsen has omitted *all* question of finance from his thirteen dramas." Stanislaus took it upon himself to object, "Maybe there are some people who are not so preoccupied about money as you are." "Maybe so, by God," said his brother, "but I'd like to take twenty-five lessons from one of those chaps."

Given a writer so convinced that old ways would not do for him, *Ulysses* was from the start designed to break with precedents. "The task I set myself technically in writing a book from eighteen different points of view and in as many styles, all apparently unknown or undiscovered by my fellow tradesmen, that and the nature of the legend chosen would be enough to upset anyone's mental balance," Joyce (whose mental balance was not upset) confided to Harriet Weaver. In this book he set himself as many difficulties as he could, knowing that his genius would be equal to them. There is the title itself, so abrupt in its insistence on a mythical background, which however is never mentioned as it was in *A Portrait of the Artist.* The author's silence about it is intimidating, yet the relation to the Odyssey is problematic, and its intensity varies from chapter to chapter, or even from page to page. Joyce felt at liberty to deal with Homer as highhandedly as Virgil had done, keeping the basic typology but varying and omitting and adding as his own book required. In the first episodes he realized his ambition of rendering the thousand complexities in the mind, and for the first time in literature we have all the lapses and bursts of attention, hesitations, half-recollections, distractions, sudden accesses or flaggings of sexual interest, feelings of hunger or nausea, somnolence, sneezing, thoughts about money, responses to the clouds and sunlight, along with the complications of social behavior and work. Joyce's power is shown not only in the density of sensations, but in the poetry and humor that infuse the principal characters and in the spirited irony of the narrator. Yet to mention these characteristics is to be put in mind of others. There is an extraordinary counterpoint between the first three chapters dealing with Stephen Dedalus and the next three dealing with Bloom. It is not only the implicit parallel of their responses at the same hours of the day, but the inner nature of the incidents that are described. So at the start of the first chapter, Buck Mulligan, holding a shaving bowl as if it were a chalice, claims to be transubstantiating the lather in it into the body and blood of Christ. Bloom makes an unspoken derisive commentary on this miracle when, at the end of the fourth chapter, he has a bowel movement and so in effect transubstantiates food into feces. Stephen ponders the way that states and churches alike have engaged in persecutions and sadistic wars, while Bloom thinks about the masochism which attracts devotees to confess and ask for punishment. A recognition of sado-masochism seems to bind the characters together, though they have not yet met. Then Stephen, as he walks along the strand and sees the debris heaped up by the waves, thinks darkly of the process of life as one from birth to decay to death. In the parallel passage in Bloom's morning, he attends a funeral, and is put in mind of the process from death through decay to new birth. What we thought were two parallel lines prove to be a circle.

As the book proceeds, the circle is itself questioned and sometimes mocked. And the reign of order gives way to the reign of chaos. The physical universe, so glancingly built up in all its multiplicity in the early episodes, begins to lose its plausibility. Space and time, once so distinct, are shaken almost out of recognition. The reader like the narrative is caught up in the agitations and images of the unconscious mind. Our daytime selves are almost overwhelmed by this night. Yet in all the disorder Joyce keeps as firm a hand as he had when all was order in the early chapters. At the end he gives us back our world, somewhat the worse for wear, based no longer upon primal certitude but upon affirmation in the face of doubt, as the universe hangs upon the void. And while he prided himself on his novel's physicality, and ended with a supposedly fleshly monologue, what we recognize in reading Molly Bloom's soliloquy is that she is no fleshlier than Hamlet, and that for her too the mind affects everything. The tenor of her thoughts is to acknowledge grudgingly that her husband, who recognizes her wit and musical talent and inner nature, is a better man than her lover Blazes Boylan. She pays Bloom the ultimate compliment, one rarely heard by men from women, "I saw he understood or felt what a woman is." Penelope recognizes Ulysses not by his scar but by his imagination. Although Joyce said jocularly of her that she is the flesh that always affirms, she is not to be identified with unconsciousness, or Mother Nature, or fertility. Her amorous career has been limited. She has copulated a little, she has ruminated a great deal. Bodies do not exist without minds. Molly may not be capable of impersonal thought, as Bloom is, but she has a good sharp practical intelligence. She is in fact cerebral too—a great and unexpected tribute from a writer who in life said many unpleasant things about women.

Joyce thought of his books as way stations on a psychic journey. His last book, *Finnegans Wake,* was an even more "extravagant excursion into forbidden territory," since it invaded the region of language itself, a region which other novelists had left inviolate. Dante obliged Italian literature to use the vernacular instead of Latin. Joyce's invention of *Finnegans-Wake*-ese was not intended to change literature so fundamentally, though it has had its imitators. Rather he wished to find an adequate medium to describe the world of night, the world of dream, the world of the unconscious, the world of madness. In such an atmosphere neither shapes nor events nor words could be intact. As he wrote in a letter, "One great part of every human existence is passed in a state which cannot be rendered sensible by the use of wideawake language, cutanddry grammar and goahead plot." Every person experiences this other state, but Joyce also envisaged a "universal history" in which he would represent the night world of humanity. This night world had always been associated with dark fantasies, but no one had described its work. The principal work of the night shift of humanity—meaning its involuntary, accidental, half-conscious labor, is the perpetual decreation and re-creation of language. The tongue slips, no one knows why. We go to sleep speaking Latin and wake up speaking French. Words break up, combine with words mysteriously imported from other languages, play tricks upon their own components. In the twinkling of a closed eye a red rose becomes a red nose, a phoenix becomes a finish, a funeral becomes a funforall. Joyce insisted that he was working strictly in accordance with the laws of phonetics, the only difference being that he accomplished in one fictional night what might take hundreds of years to occur through gradual linguistic change. He commented to a friend, Jacques Mercanton, "I reconstruct the life of the night the way the Demiurge goes about his creation, on the basis of a mental scenario that never varies. The only difference is that I obey laws I have not chosen. And he?"

(He did not continue.) When people complained that the puns he was obliged by his scenario to use were trivial he made the famous retort, "Yes, some of my means are trivial, and some are quadrivial." When they said his puns were childish, he accepted the supposed blame with alacrity. He prided himself on not having grown up. His voice, he said, had never changed in adolescence. "It's because I've not developed. If I had matured, I wouldn't be so committed to the *folie* of writing *Work in Progress*." Keeping the child in the man gave him access to the universe which adults repressed.

In these ways Joyce radicalized literature, so that it would never recover. He reconstituted narrative, both external and internal; he changed our conception of daytime consciousness and of nighttime unconsciousness. He made us reconsider language as a product and prompter of unconscious imaginings. These did not come to him as experiments or as innovations; he did not regard himself as an experimenter. Rather they were solutions to the literary and intellectual problems he set himself.

Yet though his determination to change the way we think about ourselves and others as well as the way we read required the most elaborate methods, Joyce always insisted—to use a Dantean pun—that his means were one thing, his meaning another. Complication was not in itself a good. "Can you not see the simplicity which is at the back of all my disguises?" he asked his wife before they eloped together. He objected to slavishness and ignobility; he thought they were fostered by conventional notions of heroism, which turned people into effigies rather than men and women. He wished them to know themselves as they really were, not as they were taught by church and state to consider themselves to be. He gave dignity to the common life that we all share. As he wrote to his brother, "Anyway my opinion is that if I put down a bucket into my own soul's well, sexual department, I draw up Griffith's and Ibsen's and Skeffington's and Bernard Vaughan's and St. Aloysius' and Shelley's and Renan's water along with my own. And I am going to do that in my novel (inter alia) and plank the bucket down before the shades and substances above mentioned to see how they like it: and if they don't like it I can't help them." Yet he was not impervious to those other qualities also held in common, moments of exaltation and lyricism as important as they were infrequent.

He made no personal claims. "A man of small virtue, inclined to extravagance and alcoholism" was how he described himself to the psychologist Jung. He disclaimed genius, disclaimed imagination, only asserted that when he was writing his mind was as nearly normal as possible (November 10, 1907). He wished to give his contemporaries, especially his Irish ones, a good look at themselves in his polished looking glass — as he said — but not to destroy them. They must know themselves to become freer and more alive. Shear away adhesion to conventions and shibboleths, and what have we left? More, I think, than Lear's forked animal. We have the language-making and -using capacity, we have affections and disaffections, we have also humor, through which we tumble to our likeness with others. That likeness lies in sad as well as joyful moments. The province of literature, as Joyce and his hero Stephen Dedalus both define it with unaccustomed fervor, is the eternal affirmation of the spirit of man, suffering and rollicking. We can shed what he called "laughtears" as his writings confront us with this spectacle.

James Joyce, ca. 1933. *Prints and Photographs Division.*

OTHER PUBLICATIONS ON LITERATURE AVAILABLE FROM THE LIBRARY OF CONGRESS

The following publications, based on lectures presented at the Library of Congress, are available free from the Library of Congress, Central Services Division, Washington, D.C. 20540. When ordering, please provide the title, author, and date of publication.

CARL SANDBURG by Mark Van Doren. With a bibliography of Sandburg materials in the collections of the Library of Congress. 1969. 83 p.

CHAOS AND CONTROL IN POETRY, a lecture by Stephen Spender. 1966. 14 p.

THE INSTANT OF KNOWING by Josephine Jacobsen. 1974. 14 p.

LITERARY LECTURES PRESENTED AT THE LIBRARY OF CONGRESS. 1973. 602 p.

"The Theme of the Joseph Novels" by Thomas Mann, "The War and the Future" by Thomas Mann, "Germany and the Germans" by Thomas Mann, "Nietzsche's Philosophy in the Light of Contemporary Events" by Thomas Mann, "From Poe to Valéry" by T.S. Eliot, "Goethe and Democracy" by Thomas Mann, "The Great Grasp of Unreason" by R.P. Blackmur, "The Techniques of Trouble" by R.P. Blackmur, "Irregular Metaphysics" by R.P. Blackmur, "Contemplation" by R.P. Blackmur, "George Bernard Shaw: Man of the Century" by Archibald Henderson, "The Biographical Novel" by Irving Stone, "Remarks on the Novel" by John O'Hara, "The Historical Novel" by MacKinlay Kantor, "New Poets and Old Muses" by John Crowe Ransom, "The Present State of Poetry" by Delmore Schwartz, "The Two Knowledges: An Essay on a Certain Resistance" by John Hall Wheelock, "Robert Burns" by Robert Hillyer, "Lines of Force in French Poetry" by Pierre Emmanuel, "Alfred Edward Housman" by Cleanth Brooks, "The House of Poe" by Richard Wilbur, "Willa Cather" by Leon Edel, "Latest Trends in French Prose" by Alain Bosquet, "Crossing the Zero Point: German Literature Since World War II" by Hans Egon Holthusen, "The Modern German Mind: The Legacy of Nietzsche" by Erich Heller, "Russian Soviet Literature Today" by Marc Slonim, "Chinese Letters Since the Literary Revolution (1917)" by Lin Yutang, "The Progress of Realism in the Italian Novel" by Giose Rimanelli, "The Contemporary Literature of Spain" by Arturo Torres-Rioseco, "The Imagination as Verb" by Stephen Spender, "The Organic, the Orchidaceous, the Intellectualized" by Stephen Spender, "Imagination Means Individuation" by Stephen Spender, "Recent American Fiction" by Saul Bellow, "Edwin Arlington Robinson" by Louis Untermeyer, "Hidden Name and Complex Fate: A Writer's Experience in the U.S." by Ralph Ellison, "American Poet?" by Karl Shapiro, "Ways of Misunderstanding Poetry" by Reed Whittemore.

LOUISE BOGAN: A WOMAN'S WORDS by William Jay Smith. With a bibliography. 1971. 81 p.

METAPHOR AS PURE ADVENTURE by James Dickey. 1968. 20 p.

Portrait of a Poet: Hans Christian Andersen and his Fairytales by Erik Haugaard. 1973. 17 p.

Randall Jarrell by Karl Shapiro. With a bibliography of Jarrell materials in the collections of the Library of Congress. 1967. 47 p.

The Reasons for Poetry and the Reason for Criticism by William Meredith. 1982. 36 p.

Robert Frost: Lectures on the Centennial of his Birth. 1975. 74 p.

"In- and Outdoor Schooling: Robert Frost and the Classics" by Helen Bacon, "Toward the Source: The Self-Realization of Robert Frost, 1911-1912" by Peter Davison, "Robert Frost's 'Enigmatical Reserve': The Poet as Teacher and Preacher" by Robert Pack, "Inner Weather: Robert Frost as a Metaphysical Poet" by Allen Tate.

Saint-John Perse: Praise and Presence by Pierre Emmanuel. With a bibliography. 1971. 82 p.

Spinning the Crystal Ball: Some Guesses at the Future of American Poetry by James Dickey. 1967. 22 p.

The Translation of Poetry. Address by Allen Tate and panel discussion presented at the International Poetry Festival held at the Library of Congress, April 13-15, 1970. 1972. 40 p.

Two Lectures. 1973. 31 p.

"Leftovers: a CARE Package" by William Stafford and "From Anne to Marianne: Some Women in American Poetry" by Josephine Jacobsen.

Wallace Stevens: The Poetry of Earth by A. Walton Litz. 1981. 15 p.

Walt Whitman: Man, Poet, Philosopher. 1955, reissued 1969. 53 p.

"The Man" by Gay Wilson Allen, "The Poet" by Mark Van Doren, "The Philosopher" by David Daiches.

COLOPHON

Composition:	Acorn Press, Rockville, Maryland, and General Typographers, Washington, D.C.
Text Paper:	Hopper Sunray Vellum, natural white, 70 pound text
Cover Paper:	Strathmore Grandee, Biscay green, 80 pound cover
Printing:	2,000 copies printed by Printing, Inc., Washington, D.C.
Design:	John Michael
About the Type:	The text is set in Trump Medieval Roman and Italic, designed by Georg Trump. The title, heads, and page numbers are hand set in American Uncial, designed by Victor Hammer, who was born 100 years ago in Vienna, Austria.